Date Due

MAR 1 8 1986			
OCT 30 '06			

BRO
DART   PRINTED IN U.S.A.

40 Million Schoolbooks
Can't Be Wrong

40 MILLION SCHOOLBOOKS CAN'T BE WRONG

Myths in American History

BY L. ETHAN ELLIS

MACMILLAN PUBLISHING CO., INC.
New York
COLLIER MACMILLAN PUBLISHERS
London

ACKNOWLEDGMENT: Excerpts on pages *vii* and 94 from *Daughter of Time* by Josephine Tey are reprinted by permission of the publisher, Macmillan Publishing Co., Inc. Copyright © 1951 by Elizabeth MacKintosh.

PICTURE CREDITS

The Bettmann Archives, 23, 33, 44, 69
Herblock Cartoons, 83
Library of Congress, 5, 13, 57
The Metropolitan Museum of Art (Gift of John S. Kennedy, 1897), 1

1 2 3 4 5 6 7 8 9 10

Library of Congress Cataloging in Publication Data
Ellis, Lewis Ethan, date
  40 million schoolbooks can't be wrong.

Bibliography: p. Includes index.
1. United States—History—Juvenile literature.
[1. United States—History] I. Title.
E178.3.E493 973 75–14227 ISBN 0–02–733450–3

To Beth, Robby, and David

"Forty million school books can't be wrong," Grant said after a little. *"Can't they?"*

—Josephine Tey,
Daughter of Time

CONTENTS

Acknowledgments

The author wishes to thank Dr. George P. Schmidt, Professor Emeritus in American History, Douglass College, Rutgers University, for reading and suggesting changes in the manuscript of this book.
Thanks also to David L. Reuther of the publisher's editorial staff.

Introduction

WASHINGTON CROSSING THE DELAWARE
BY EMANUEL LEUTZÉ (1851)

*How myths get started—this well-known painting
gives a daytime version of Washington's night-time
crossing in 1776. It also shows the Stars and Stripes,
which became our flag only in June, 1777.*

If you have been brought up to think that history books tell "the truth, the whole truth, and nothing but the truth," it may come as a real shock to learn that this is often not the case. Some history books omit events unfavorable to their own point of view, while twisting the significance of the facts they do present. A great many books contain half-truths, distortions, and much general misinformation, and many others are guilty of perpetuating certain basic myths and legends—events which are simply not true, but which have been repeated for so many years that almost everyone takes them for granted. The myth of the savage Indian is a good example of the above; the legend of George Washington and the cherry tree is another.

You might well ask: why are myths and legends, half-truths and distortions so common in our history books, or, if the facts are known, why aren't they reported accurately? The answer to this question is a complicated one, and a great many people are involved.

Most of us believe in something which others may oppose. In defending oneself there is always the tendency to exaggerate, to "draw the long bow." On a large scale this process of exaggeration can lead to a myth. Take slavery, for example. At first it was widespread throughout the country. In some parts it became unprofitable, but cotton culture fixed it in the South. In the North, abolitionists condemned slavery on moral grounds and tried to do away with it. In the ensuing controversy, both sides said and wrote many things which were not true. Eventually the distortions hardened into myths, and even today it is still difficult to view this era objectively.

Politicians striving to get elected or reelected seldom underestimate their own virtues. If they are elected, their accomplishments tend to multiply in their own eyes and those of their supporters; a favorable press emphasizes their achievements and presently they find their way into the history books. Unless politicians are openly inept or crooked, these favorable pictures tend to be fixed on the historical landscape.

Newspapermen write for an immediate audience and therefore must attract the attention of their readers. Sensationalism and exaggeration are tricks of the trade which can and often do perpetuate themselves. Radio, television, and motion pictures have conditioned us to accept condensed and predigested history—but condensing must be done with great care to avoid distortion. The stereotyped cowboy and Indian movie, for example, did much to perpetuate the myth of the bloodthirsty savage.

Novelists sometimes find themselves exaggerating the facts, whether to prove a point or for literary effect, and often their writings help to create a distorted picture of reality. One example is the falsely harsh picture of the Puritans drawn in Nathaniel Hawthorne's *The Scarlet Letter*.

Nor are the writers of history guiltless. In earlier days, provincialism often clouded their outlook. A New Englander writing about a South which he had never seen, or an Eastern cosmopolitan writing about the Western frontier, was likely to write with a bias that could easily be converted into a myth. Even today, when most of us travel a great deal, these sectional and personal biases are not easy to avoid.

Writers of history, whether they admit it or not, are influenced by the temper of their own time, and tend to reflect a prevailing political or economic attitude. This tendency increases when succeeding generations of writers accept, as they sometimes have, the conclusions of their predecessors. Often writers of textbooks do not keep up with the latest research. Indeed, they have been known to be deliberately deceitful, writing one history of the Civil War for books to be marketed in the North, and a different one for those to be sold in the South.

Now, a word about "revisionism." I used to tell my students, not more than half facetiously, that historians keep themselves in business by revising one another's findings. Scholars always need to demonstrate their skills. One popular way to do this is to show that previous writers on a subject have, for lack of information or insight, created or perpetuated points of view which are false. This is the process of historical revisionism. Some history teachers (none of yours, of course) fail to keep up with revisionist books. Too often they absorb a particular point of view from their professors in college or graduate school, fit it comfortably into their teaching routines, and live with it happily ever after. This means that they are unfamiliar with the conclusions of the most recent studies and thus are a step or more behind the times.

Once a myth has been created, its perpetuation is relatively easy. The printed page carries an authority all its own. "I read it in a book" tends to convince a lot of people, especially if the author is well known or well liked. Also, there is a time-lag between what historians examine and what is going on around them. So, once a myth has been created, it gains a sort of prestige which is difficult to overcome.

And so it goes. This book is an attempt to redress some of the imbalances in American history—to show where exaggeration, personal bias, sectional patriotism, and other factors have resulted in distortions of the record. Reading this book will not, I hope, end in cynicism or disillusionment, for that is not my intent. We need not be unhappy to learn that our country has not always been right or that its historians have not all been perfect, either.

1. The Colonial Period

American cartoon on the proposal to establish an episcopate of the Church of England in the colonies.

England, France, Spain and Portugal all joined in the voyages of discovery in the late fifteenth and sixteenth centuries. These had revealed North and South America as fairly permanent obstacles to reaching the riches of the Far East. Only later did Europeans begin to look on the two continents as ends in themselves. Then, in the seventeenth century, a period of colonization saw the nations staking out vast claims to this new territory.

British interest came to focus on what is now the United States, and eventually thirteen colonies were established along the Atlantic seaboard. Englishmen were unprepared for what they were to encounter during those years of settlement and occupation, and their experiences were often difficult.

The Myth of Instantaneous Hostility

When the era of discovery opened, European pioneers found the Indians occupying most of North America. The Indians had been here for thousands of years and possessed political and social organizations which were often quite highly developed.

The old chestnut which says that the Pilgrims stepped off Plymouth Rock, "fell first on their knees and then on the aborigines [Indians]," is only a joke. The Indians were highly useful to the relatively sophisticated Europeans, furnishing them with knowledge of the ways of the forest. No explorer or settler was familiar with the environment in which he found himself upon landing. The Indian's willingness to share his knowledge of forest trails and survival techniques may well have made the difference between success and failure for early European colonies.

This early harmony was too good to last. The Indian had the curious notion that the forest belonged to him and that it should continue as a hunting preserve to maintain his way of life. The colonists, accustomed to an agricultural society, soon began to convert the forest into fields. The resulting friction grew into open hostility, which was bad for both sides but particularly for the Indian, who was doomed to years of warfare and humiliation. The myth of instantaneous hostility, however, is no more than a myth.

The English Migration

Why did seventeenth-century Englishmen leave Europe for America? In part they were continuing, as settlers, what their sixteenth-century ancestors had begun as explorers. Beyond this, simple explanations will not do for all colonists nor for all periods of colonization. Here we shall confine our attention to those Englishmen who came to Virginia (1607) and to those who came to Plymouth (1620s), or to Massachusetts Bay (1630s) as part of the so-called "Great Migration."

The stereotyped reasons given for migration have been God, in New England, and Mammon, or worldly goods, in Virginia. Neither is completely correct. Indeed, one factor only lately receiving sufficient emphasis is that Englishmen were often more interested in *leaving* an old place than in *going* to a new one.

Most of those who went first to Virginia were the poor, who saw no means of bettering their lot in England. The Pilgrims who came to Plymouth had already emigrated once, to Holland, where things grew less and less to their liking. They came to America to seek refuge in yet another country. The point here is that many Englishmen simply wanted out.

Americans who travel in present-day Virginia visit such spacious and dignified examples of the Southern past as Monticello and Williamsburg, reflecting a way of life both gracious and elegant. Most movies show a Virginia of economic well-being, peopled by bewigged and heavily powdered aristocrats—a vision to which earlier novels contributed heavily. Unfortunately, conditions in early Virginia give no support to such a picture.

Most early settlers were craftsmen and merchants. Only 35 of Jamestown's 105 original settlers were entitled to be called gentlemen. These gentlemen were a dissipated crew, and most of them died within a few months. Those who were left were mostly merchants who adjusted to agriculture with the development of a tobacco culture. They worked hard and had a rough time of it, with long periods of little profit. Only generations later did the families arrive whose descendants became the pre–Civil War aristocrats.

What, then, were the Virginia colonists after? As merchants-turned-farmers, they were of course interested in profits. But it is important to point out that there was also a distinctly religious aspect to Virginia settlement. The

Puritan emphasis on religion was by no means confined to Plymouth. As Professor Perry Miller has pointed out, the settlement of Virginia was not a "purely business proposition." By looking at the colonization propaganda literature, Professor Miller has found much evidence that religion, including conversion of the Indians, was "the really energizing power in this settlement."

As in Virginia, both economic and religious factors played their parts in the settling of New England. The Pilgrims came to Plymouth in 1620, after spending twelve years as emigrants in the Netherlands. Although the Dutch had made them welcome, they had had to contend with a foreign language, with alien customs, with a strange and second-rate school system, with religious differences among their hosts, and with peril to their sense of English nationality.

Although the Dutch did not mistreat them, the Puritans felt themselves aliens, and increasingly poor aliens at that. It seems to have been this feeling of alienation, the fear of losing their identity as Englishmen, and a desire to improve their limited economic status that triggered the move to Plymouth. It would be unfair to say that these good Calvinists entirely ignored the religious motive, but it is clear that this was not dominant.

It was otherwise with the Great Migration, which brought large numbers of Puritans to the Massachusetts Bay Colony. Life was hard in the England of the 1620s and 1630s. Housing was poor and fuel was costly; land was scarce, as was food; prices and taxes were high; a vast number of punishments were enforced for the commission of minor crimes. The people most affected by these economic and social burdens had no voice in government to enable them to improve their lot in life. In addition, the Church of England was making things very uncomfortable for the Puritans.

On the basis of accumulated evidence, it is clear that thousands of Puritans emigrated with the hope of improving their own religious lot, and, and at the same time, of being "a beacon of hope for other men," i.e., the Indians. This is not to say that the prospect of free land and better living conditions was unimportant. But it can be said that the religious factor was uppermost in the minds of thousands of the Englishmen who made up the Great Migration.

One other factor, propaganda, was of considerable importance in this Great Migration. The sermons of English Puritan preachers of the late 1620s and the 1630s contain repeated references to the virtues of America, urging the faithful to move there for the good of their bodies as well as their souls. Merchants, too, had learned that there was profit in carrying men as well as goods across the Atlantic, and they hired recruiters to fill the uncomfortable berths of their heavily laden ships. Thus, religious, social, and economic factors worked together to speed Englishmen to Massachusetts, with religion, in the broad sense, being a dominant factor for the first time.

The Myth of the Puritanical Puritans

A twentieth-century student, trying to picture the typical Puritan as he lived in the Plymouth and Massachusetts Bay Colonies, will probably draw a fairly dreary picture. His

Puritan is likely to emerge as a long-faced, somberly dressed, and apparently joyless individual, who lived in dread of any departure from established custom in this life and in fear of Hell in the next. This is an unfortunate exaggeration.

Several factors have contributed to this distortion. A large influence should be credited to Nathaniel Hawthorne, whose novel, *The Scarlet Letter* (1850), drew a grim picture of Puritan life in general, while telling the story of a young matron who bore a son by the local pastor during her husband's two-year absence. This literary myth was repeated by other artists, for example, the statue by Augustus Saint-Gaudens, depicting the stereotyped Puritan. More recently, in the 1920s, H. L. Mencken used the pages of *The American Mercury* to connect his version of the "Puritan ethic" with the Eighteenth Amendment to the Constitution, which interfered, unsuccessfully, with Mencken's right to drink alcoholic beverages.

In truth, the Puritans emerge from fairer examination as much less forbidding and considerably more human individuals. There is no doubt that they were strait-laced. Their laws punished anyone caught in sexual indiscretions. However, Puritan church records show that those who thus entertained themselves without getting caught, and who later confessed, were not punished by the law and were taken into the bosom of the church without penalty.

Church membership was required for voting in a Massachusetts Town Meeting. However, the church member who voted in Massachusetts would not have had the same privilege in most of Europe and in many of the other colonies, so that the religious qualification was not as limiting as it seems today.

The Puritans obviously took their religion seriously, but they were not obsessed by it. It has been noted above that in Massachusetts, religion was a major factor in migration. It would have indeed been strange if the emigrant's soul was not one of his major concerns. This is witnessed by the fact that Puritans could listen to long sermons in unheated churches, and by the severity of a good many of their regulations. It is not fair to condemn the Puritan for these regulations, which were typical of the time and later softened in practice.

What, then, shall we say of the Puritans? Perhaps it would be fair to characterize them as people of great boldness who gambled their lives for the right to live them in their own way. While stricter than some, the Puritan lifestyle was still a fairly reasonable approach to the problem of living and one probably well adapted to the difficult conditions in the New World.

2. The American Revolution

Colonial opposition to the Stamp Act.

Since the early days of colonization, the British "family" had come to consist of England, the "parent," and thirteen "children," spread for fifteen hundred miles along the east coast of North America. These children were sharply different in many respects, but they all faced what we can look back on as a painful period of adjustment.

The Myth of the Oppressive Parent

The traditional relationship between Mother Country and colonies is known today as "mercantilism." In non-technical terms, mercantilism was a system under which the colonies were founded through parental initiative, protected by parental strength, and ruled by parental authority. To this authority the colonies owed certain obligations. In return they received parental support and protection against outside enemies.

The burden of this authority rested fairly lightly on the colonies. The Woolens Act of 1699, the Hat Act of 1732, and the Iron Act of 1750 put limits on colonial manufactures, which could not possibly have supplied the local market. The Navigation Acts, enacted between 1650 and 1700, laid some moderately costly burdens on colonial trade, but under no circumstances could all of the goods have been carried in colonial ships.

On balance, the Acts helped the family without unduly restricting its junior members. They did produce some colonial grumbling, but this fell far short of a real crisis.

The time was coming, however, when the family would begin to feel the strain.

The triggering factor was a series of Anglo-French wars for colonial supremacy. These "French and Indian" wars were fought off and on from 1689 to 1763, and ended with complete British victory and elimination of France as a colonial rival. They were fought with British troops and money, on behalf of both the Mother Country and the colonies. Colonial participation in the local defense was seldom very enthusiastic, but it contributed to an emerging sense of selfhood and colonial independence.

In 1763 Britain was a bankrupt winner; the wars had been won but not paid for. The maturing colonies, however, found themselves relieved of the fear of the French and their Indian allies. It was this combination of parental poverty and approaching colonial maturity that produced a family crisis in the British Empire.

In Britain itself, a power struggle had been going on between Parliament and King, with the balance gradually tilting in favor of the former. The colonies had been founded under royal authority. Now Parliament sought colonial assistance in bearing the burden of a postwar debt, about half of it incurred on behalf of the colonies themselves. The colonies were not slow to resent this "taxation," as they called it. To them it was a new imposition. The laws mentioned in an earlier paragraph were enacted to direct the course of trade and manufactures, not to raise revenue.

Each new piece of revenue legislation—the Sugar Act (1764), the Stamp Act (1765), the Townshend Acts (1767), the Tea Act (1773), and the Coercive or Intoler-

able Acts (1774)—provoked an increasingly strong reaction. The growing colonial hostility to these "imperial"
taxes led eventually to the Continental Congresses and,
finally, to armed revolt.

The point to stress here is that the British legislation
contained no evil design on colonial freedom, and calling
it "tyranny" was as much a myth then as it is today. The
fact is that Britain's attempt to assert a previously unexer-
cised power ran up against a colonial attitude of increasing
maturity and self-sufficiency which refused to be placed
in such a position of inferiority.

After studying some four hundred colonial pamphlets,
Professor Bernard Bailyn has concluded that the Americans
felt themselves the objects of a British "conspiracy" aimed
at destroying their liberties. Though he and other historians have found little foundation for these fears, they were
very real to eighteenth-century Americans, and their influence must be kept in mind.

One other matter should be mentioned in this account
of the taxation question—the taxes themselves were actually very light, both in relation to earlier burdens on the
colonists and to taxes on Englishmen at home. It has been
calculated that the earlier taxes on the colonists were five
times as heavy as those sought in the immediate pre-revolu-
tionary period. In 1775 Lord North told the House of
Commons that Englishmen at home were being taxed fifty
times as much per person as were the Americans. From
this it is clear that the colonials were wounded less in their
pocketbooks than in their pride—the latter was by this
time as tender as the former.

We must conclude, then, as did John Adams, that "the

American Revolution was started in the hearts and minds of men," rather than by an oppressive Parliament or by King George III. This change had been developing for generations; it was merely triggered by the alleged British "tyranny."

The Boston Tea Party

Between the revolution which was occurring in the hearts and minds of men, and the war which began with Lexington and Concord, came the Boston Tea Party. In 1775 the principal sign of imperial "oppression" was the threepence per pound tax on tea, retained from the Townshend Acts in an effort to create the illusion of British authority over the colonies. In reality, expert smugglers made it unnecessary for the colonists to worry much about this tax. At this low point of Anglo-American tensions, Parliament unintentionally reignited colonial suspicions of the Mother Country and set the stage for another myth of British cruelty.

The British East India Company had been so badly mismanaged that it was on the verge of bankruptcy. To prevent this, the Tea Act of 1773 permitted the Company to send tea directly from the Far East to the colonies, avoiding the stop in Britain which had previously been required, and so eliminating shipping and handling costs. This made it possible to sell the tea so cheaply as to endanger the smugglers' livelihood. There is no evidence of evil intent on the part of Parliament.

Colonial agitators fabricated evidence of evil intent;

this threatened injustice gave them the opportunity they needed to attack their parent land. They voiced strong protests at such oppression, and this resulted in various measures to prevent it from taking place. Six hundred thousand pounds of tea presently arrived offshore. At Charleston the tea was seized and stored; New Yorkers and Philadelphians persuaded the ships' captains to turn back for home. A mob of Bostonians, some wearing Indian clothing, dumped their tea into the harbor. This was the Boston Tea Party, news of which was a great surprise in London.

The consequences were tremendous. The British retaliated with the Intolerable Acts. These in turn helped the agitators to whip up more revolutionary sentiment. The First Continental Congress (September, 1774) was followed by the Second (May, 1775), the latter held under the echo of the musket-fire at Lexington and Concord.

The Myth of the Unanimous Uprising

After Lexington and Concord, and the Declaration of Independence which followed, there was no turning back. The colonies were no longer striving for a place within the British Empire but for a place outside it. American writers have long held the view that this was a unanimous and spontaneous effort. Witness Henry Wadsworth Longfellow's assertion that Paul Revere was

> *Ready to ride and spread the alarm*
> *Through every Middlesex village and farm,*
> *For the country folk to be up and to arm.*

Or George Bancroft's testimony that "the people of the continent with irresistible energy obeyed one general impulse, as the earth in the spring listens to the command of nature, and without the appearance of effort burst forth to life in perfect harmony." This was, of course, an exaggeration, but it rapidly became a myth in its own right. All of this would have seemed rather strange to George Washington, who at one point complained bitterly of "the egregious want of public spirit" among his troops.

The emergence of a group called the Loyalists proved that many colonists were neither patriots nor rebels. Many of these Loyalists would swallow their distaste for revolution and remain Americans. Others stood by their true feelings and left the colonies, abandoning their property and often splitting their families in order to retain the name of Englishmen.

Who became Loyalists, and why? Although they came from all walks of life, it appears that professionals and officeholders, large landowners, merchants, Anglicans, and Quakers formed the backbone of the group. These people had a stake, both economic and political, in the British Empire—a stake which they thought would be endangered if the patriots gained the upper hand.

Many Loyalists never had to declare themselves openly. They were "reluctant revolutionaries," and kept their ideas to themselves as much as possible, often to the end of the war. As the war dragged on, however, more and more of them were forced out into the open.

How many colonists were Loyalists? As we have just seen, reliable statistics are not available. In 1814 John

Adams, who had lived among them, estimated that one third of the colonists had opposed the Revolution. Of course not all of these became Loyalists. Wallace Brown, the leading authority on the subject, has estimated that from 13 to 30 percent of the white population (including women and children) were active Loyalists. There is no way to count the passive ones mentioned above.

Finally, what became of them? The passive Loyalists, of course, kept their ideas to themselves and remained at home. The more militant or forthright ones emigrated. These emigrants probably totaled one hundred thousand or more, many of whom came back in the British army to fight the colonists. The Loyalists settled, eventually, in what are now the Canadian provinces of New Brunswick and Nova Scotia, and added an active British element to French-speaking Quebec, at that time also under the British flag.

The War of Independence

No one can successfully dispute the quality of George Washington's character and leadership. A heroic but historically inaccurate picture of his crossing the Delaware (painted in 1851) has created an exaggerated impression of him as a military genius, which he was not. Washington was a Virginian of high social position and some lower-level military experience. He was brought north to command a ragtag army at a time when military and political affairs called for a man of his qualities. As a soldier, his defeats outnumbered his victories, save for the Yorktown campaign, and even here French soldiers outnumbered his own on land and a French fleet probably tilted the balance in his favor.

Why, then, did the war go as it did? Washington's moral leadership, mentioned above, was undoubtedly an important factor. Other generals, too, contributed a large share of military competence. And, as is often the case, new parties entered the fray. By the early 1780s Spain and Holland were openly belligerent on the American side, and a loosely organized Armed Neutrality of the North, under Russian leadership, was making things unpleasant for Britain. On top of all this, France had formally declared for the American cause. Small wonder then that Britain, after half a decade of waging a transatlantic war, was willing to consider an end to hostilities.

The role of France, like that of Washington, has been clothed in tradition, much of it exaggerated. The assistance of French matériel had been essential in the war's early stages—French powder touched off far more than half of American fire power in 1776–77. Individual Frenchmen, such as the Marquis de Lafayette, as well as others not so well known, lent their prestige, their influence, and in some cases their considerable military ability, to the patriot cause. In 1778 a formal alliance between France and the Americans promised a common effort to win the war. It also established that neither party would make peace or truce without previously obtaining the consent of the other. French assistance at Yorktown, already mentioned, was continued in considerable measure throughout the struggle. All this created a feeling of debt toward the French which still existed when an American officer, arriving in France in 1917, dramatically announced: "La-fayette, we are here."

What are the facts? First, France did not lend her assistance to the United States on idealistic grounds alone. Indeed, American independence was quite secondary to the opportunity to humiliate France's cross-Channel enemy. We need shed few tears, then, over a debt to France left unpaid until World War I.

Secondly, was French assistance the deciding factor in the American victory? This is, of course, a difficult question to answer with certainty. However, Professor Richard B. Morris has argued that the war could probably have been won without French aid, important though this was, *and* that French failure at crucial points contributed to extending the war and, perhaps, prevented an Anglo-American settlement earlier than the Treaty of Paris in 1783.

3. The Early Nation

Merchants tried to smuggle goods out of the country during the Embargo Act (spelled backward— O Grab Me). The turtle symbolizes oppression by the federal government.

Americans have lived under two written constitutions. The first, the Articles of Confederation, was a wartime document, presented by the Continental Congress in 1777 but not ratified by all the states until 1781. The second, the Constitution of the United States, drafted at Philadelphia in 1787, and since frequently amended, seems likely to continue to serve us for the foreseeable future.

The Myth of the Critical Period

The Articles of Confederation were created by a Congress representing the thirteen newly independent states, which were engaged in reordering their affairs and in conducting a long-drawn-out and often desperately fought war. We would hardly expect such a body to impose a high degree of central authortity. The facts bear this out.

The Articles represented a minimum of centralized control while attempting to guarantee a maximum of state independence. They created a Congress which lacked a number of powers essential to efficient central government, such as taxing, borrowing, and regulating foreign commerce. In the terms of political scientists, they created a "federal" as opposed to a "national" government.

To what extent did this form of government lead to the change of system represented by the Constitution? Here there have been a number of different opinions, and the issue is still in contention.

The first major study of the question was John Fiske's *The Critical Period in American History, 1783–1789*

(1888). Fiske vividly portrayed a dismal period in which everything possible went wrong and everything wrong was the fault of the central government (or lack of it) under the Articles. The government, he pointed out, was powerless; the nation's economy was virtually bankrupt; its position vis-à-vis its domestic and foreign creditors was desperate; and foreign nations were taking advantage of American ineffectiveness in international relations. Despite sharp criticism of Fiske's methods as a historian, his book's catchy title, and much of its content, found their way into the history books and remained there for many years.

In the 1940s and 50s, Professor Merrill Jensen studied the evidence more scientifically and came to the conclusion that, while all was not rosy, neither were things as bad as Fiske had said they were. State debts, if not national, were being paid; an economic depression was on the way out; and international trade was on the upswing, leaving the mercantile classes in good shape. His studies, in fact, presented impressive evidence to show that this was a not-so-critical period.

Professor Gordon S. Wood began a third round a decade later, marshaling evidence quite as impressive as Jensen's to show that all was *not* well. One quotation from Wood must suffice: "Nearly everyone in 1787 conceded 'the weakness of the Confederation.' All 'men of reflection,' even 'the most orthodox republicans,' said [James] Madison, were alarmed by 'the existing embarrassments and mortal diseases of the Confederacy.' " This, of course, recalls Fiske's approach and shows that the argument is not yet over.

The Myth of the Saintly Founding Fathers

Regardless of the effectiveness of government under the Articles, a Convention at Philadelphia (1787) drafted a new document to replace them. Why this development? It came because a determined group of men concluded that the existing "federal" type of association was inadequate and tried, successfully as events would prove, to replace it with the stronger "national" government represented by the Constitution. The character, motives, and methods of these men, and of their unsuccessful opponents, have been examined by many historians, with widely differing conclusions.

As long as the Confederation was seen as a "critical period," it was customary to refer to the framers of the Constitution in glowing terms. Through the Constitution, it was asserted, these high-minded patriots brought order out of chaos. If not demigods, as the more enthusiastic of their admirers suggested, they could honestly be revered for unselfishly striving for the betterment of their country.

Then came Charles A. Beard. His book, *An Economic Interpretation of the Constitution of the United States* (1913), was one of the most influential and controversial ever to roll off an American press. Beard charged that the Founding Fathers were mostly conservative schemers, consciously bent on creating a strong central government to protect their own economic interests against the alleged dangers of the weak system of the Articles. Indeed, he seemed to argue that the Constitution was a counter-revolution against the will of the majority, put over by a well-organized minority in and out of the Convention.

Although Beard frankly admitted that his evidence was fragmentary, his approach proved more than a match for those who for patriotic or emotional reasons rose to attack it. From shock to incredulity, writers came to swallow more and more of the Beardian thesis and to incorporate it into their general accounts of the period.

Then came a reaction. Beard's opponents had to admit that the new government under the Constitution was stronger than the one which it had replaced. Their problem, then, was to show that this new power did not result from a conspiracy to protect the economic interests of the property-holding classes. They approached this task by making much more detailed studies of the drafting and ratification of the Constitution.

These studies, which we can only hastily summarize here, made it clear that the delegates at Philadelphia showed no such unified class objectives as Beard had suggested. On the contrary, many supported measures which went against their own alleged class interest. Moreover, the contest over ratification in the states defied Beard's neat categories of property-holders on the one hand vs. small-farmer/debtor groups on the other. Nor were the actions of particular groups in one state always identical with those of similar groups in other states. So, it seemed to these historians, economic interests and class-consciousness did *not* explain the Constitution.

How, then, can we understand the adoption of this much stronger form of government? There is no doubt, of course, that economic interests play a part in all of life.

The Founding Fathers would have been odd indeed had their system paid no heed to economic factors. Again, despite the possible virtues of the Confederation, it had equally obvious defects.

The young and forward-looking men who formed a large percentage of the "nationalists" can be pardoned for working for a stronger system of government in which they would be certain to play a considerable role. And, although some particular interests suffered, the net result of ratification was likely to prove more beneficial than otherwise. Here, then, is no counter-revolution, but a reasoned step toward a stronger government, achieved by a reasonably democratic process.

Parties and Politics

Democratic governments, strong or weak, do not run themselves. They function through political machinery of one kind or another. A myth has arisen around the history of our political machinery down to the end of the eighteenth century. This myth would have us believe that the groups which contested the framing and ratification of the Constitution—the federalists and antifederalists—had tended to disappear by the time George Washington, unanimously chosen President by the cumbersome electoral college established by the Constitution, took the oath of office in 1789.

Hardly anything could be further from the truth. Although the federalists boasted an overwhelming majority in the first Congress, the antifederalists took this as a signal to renew their efforts to establish local authority. Almost every problem, foreign or domestic, which engaged national attention during that first decade involved the federal vs. national government argument. Indeed, in one form or another, this argument still goes on today.

It would be a mistake, however, to believe that the federalists of 1787–89 were identical with the Federalist Party during the controversies of the 1790s; just as it would be incorrect to identify the antifederalists with the antifederalist Jeffersonian or Democratic-Republican Party. Finally, neither the federalists nor the antifederalists were political parties in the modern usage of that term.

First let us look at what happened to the groups which contended over the ratification of the Constitution. The antifederalists, those defeated in the fight, made their chief mission an attempt to perfect the new government whose centralization they had opposed. Even here, however, some antifederalist leaders, including Patrick Henry and Richard Henry Lee, found the weak-government leadership of the 1790s disagreeable and joined the Federalist Party. A good many federalists found the strong-government leadership of the 1790s equally uncongenial. Prominent among these was James Madison, an arch-federalist known as the "Father of the Constitution," who became a Republican. Thus the fight continued but the personnel tended to change a little.

A political party can be defined as a reasonably compact and stable group whose leaders attempt to persuade a majority of the voters to back a definite set of principles and programs at the ballot-box and in the legislature. In that case it is a mistake to claim that political parties, in our sense of the term, existed during the framing and adoption of the Constitution. Another myth would have them springing up fully fledged during the so-called "Federalist Period" (1789–1801), while George Washington and John Adams occupied the Presidency. They did emerge, but gradually, and in relation to a succession of sometimes overlapping domestic and foreign problems.

In 1789, a new government had been launched, its institutions tried out in practice and, it was hoped, its economic foundations solidly constructed. The first widespread difference of opinion emerged from the financial program which was sponsored by Alexander Hamilton, the Secretary of the Treasury. This was designed to raise revenue and to personify the authority of the central government.

Each element of this program, introduced over a number of months in 1791–92, raised anguished protests. As the programs developed, these gradually assumed a north/ south sectional aspect, as well as demonstrating a vigorous difference over the central government's power, or lack of it, to pass and enforce such centralizing legislation.

It should be noted, however, that though hostility was great, it was organized on what we would today call a *partisan*, rather than a *party* basis—in other words, there was no full-fledged party organization, but rather a reasonably, though not formally, united and somewhat sectional opposition to the Hamiltonian program.

While domestic programs furnished the arena in which federalist and antifederalist partisanship developed, foreign affairs precipitated this partisanship into full-fledged parties.

France had also undergone a great upheaval in 1789. Her great Revolution filled the hearts of other European monarchs with fear, lest the French spirit infect their people as well. This fear led to an Anglo-French war which, by 1793, had involved much of Europe and put the United States in a dilemma, in which we had to balance our obligations to France against our interest in maintaining good relations with Britain, upon which much of Hamilton's financial program depended.

The result of this balancing act was the Jay Treaty with Britain. While temporarily postponing trouble with the British, it gave France grounds for complaint that we had not lived up to our obligations under the Franco-American treaty of 1778. Thus neither party was satisfied, and our own position in relation to the European struggle remained precarious.

The Jay Treaty, as Professor Jerald A. Combs argues, completed the formation of political parties. The factions which had been arguing over various domestic matters gathered behind Hamilton in defending the treaty and behind Thomas Jefferson, the Secretary of State, in attacking it. We would now be willing to call these factions Federalists and Republicans.

4. Growing Pains

"WHAT! YOU YOUNG YANKEE-
NOODLE, STRIKE YOUR OWN
FATHER!"

*English view of American antagonism over
the Oregon boundary line.*

Americans have always been a restless people. As individuals, we have overstepped the fringes of existing settlement; as a nation, we have added territory beyond our existing legal boundaries. Sometimes these processes have proceeded simultaneously, sending Americans across North America and far out into the Pacific.

The first process, exploration, involves the "frontier." By the second process, acquisition, the United States obtained over five times its original territory, at the expense of several earlier owners. Each of these processes has produced its quota of myths.

The Myth of the Frontier

The myth of the frontier centers around Frederick Jackson Turner, whose essay, "The Influence of the Frontier in American History" (1893), touched off a controversy which is still under way. Indeed, it ranks with Charles Beard's work, mentioned earlier, among the most influential studies in the field of American history. Turner developed the thesis that our history could best be understood in terms of the frontier, where rigorous conditions produced a unique character—the American.

Turner started with the census of 1890, which said that the frontier (defined as an area populated by two persons or less per square mile) had disappeared. According to Turner, this frontier "masters the colonist. It finds him a European in dress, industries, tools, modes of travel, and thought. . . . It strips off the garments of civilization and arrays him in the hunting shirt and the moccasins. . . . Before long he has gone to planting Indian corn and plowing with a sharp stick. . . . Little by little he transforms the wilderness." And again: "[T]he advance of the frontier has meant a steady movement away from the influence of Europe, a steady growth of independence on American lines."

As Turner envisioned it, the frontier was a *process*, continually repeating itself and its distinctive characteristics. He tried to show that frontier free land acted as a safety valve to relieve recurrent pressures in the East, and produced a peculiar type of American—individualistic, self-reliant, and democratic.

Turner's thesis caught on, reflecting the temper of his time. A most persuasive and enthusiastic teacher, he inspired a whole school of writers who caught his fervor and spread his gospel. Like the master, they tended to deal in generalities more than in detailed research, and their writings elaborated his thesis at great length.

As with Beard's economic theory, Turner's thesis was soon challenged. His unfortunate use of the term "free land" gave his critics a handle, which they pumped vigorously, correctly noting that free land had been a myth during most of our history. Until the Homestead Act of 1862, national legislation had always placed a price tag of from $1.00 to $2.25 per acre on public land. If one added the cost of moving and of opening up the new land, the adjective "free" was a myth, especially when a dollar bought more than it does today.

Turner proposed (but he did not invent) the "safety-valve theory"—in times of depression, Americans "cleaned the skillet and called the dog," and went West looking for better things. It has been pretty well demonstrated by now that depressions really slowed the westward movement. Moreover, it would appear that the hard-up eastern farmer was more likely to take refuge in a nearby city than in the frontier. Professor Fred A. Shannon has estimated that the ratio of farmers-moving-to-the-city to artisans-moving-to-the-frontier was twenty to one.

Another of Turner's key assertions has been vigorously attacked—that the frontier produced a society "strong in selfishness and individualism, intolerant of experience and education, and pressing individual liberty beyond its proper bounds . . . ." Indeed, M. C. Boatright wrote, "There is no more persistent myth in American history than the myth that rugged individualism is or has been the way of American life." Boatright, indeed, presents impressive evidence to show how the principle of "mutuality" inspired many frontier group activities, such as labor, construction, and mutual protection against common enemies.

Turner's powerful argument that the frontier bred democracy has been the subject both of a vigorous attack and a fairly vigorous defense. Turner wrote that "it was only as the interior of the country developed that suffrage restrictions gradually gave way in the direction of manhood suffrage." A more recent study concludes, however, that "it is difficult to believe that the New West was unique or that it made any new contribution to the growth of suffrage democracy."

After studying the early days of the Ohio Valley states,

Professor John D. Barnhart concludes that, in this area at least, democracy assumed a distinctly American tone, and was indeed largely a product of frontier conditions—a tentative confirmation of Turner's point of view.

What shall we say of Turner and the frontier myth he helped create? First, that he was somewhat less single-minded than his opponents have suggested. He did *not* insist that the frontier alone, among such factors as urbanization, industrialization, and immigration, was the only way in which America could be interpreted. He *did* emphasize the prime importance of the frontier, as does any discoverer of a new idea.

Again, Turner was less concerned with supporting his broad and appealing generalizations than a later generation of historians. However, this is often true of pioneers in a new field, who do the spadework and leave it to later folk to fill in the gaps. As in the case of the Ohio Valley, it may indeed turn out that filling in these gaps will tend to support, rather than undermine, Turner's thesis.

The Myth of Manifest Destiny

The remarkable American appetite for territory and the speed with which the American flag was carried to the Pacific have sometimes been referred to politely as "expansionism" and less politely as "imperialism."

The word "expansionism" has relatively pure connotations. It suggests the exuberance of youth, enthusiasm for action, and a desire for self-improvement, with little or no connotation that such self-improvement might have unfavorable consequences for others. "Imperialism," on the other hand, sounds from the beginning like a dirty word. It suggests opportunism, conniving, and the use of force to gain territorial ends at the expense of others. Which of these words should we apply to the United States?

As usual, there is a difference of opinion among the so-called experts. The *New York Times* once claimed (1926) that "we cannot rightly be charged with imperialism, disguised or avowed. . . ." since down to that time we had never maintained large military or naval forces. The *Christian Science Monitor* also asserted (1927) that "there has never existed . . . in the consciousness of the American people . . . what have been popularly defined . . . as imperialistic tendencies." And the late Samuel Flagg Bemis, for years the dean of American diplomatic historians, wrote in 1949 that "if one defines imperialism as dominion over alien people, the United States can scarcely be said to have been an imperialistic nation during the nineteenth century. . . . The old Manifest Destiny was not imperialism."

Equally and perhaps more impressive authorities, however, may be found on the other side. Hardly was the ink dry on the new Constitution than Jedediah Morse wrote (in 1789), "Here Genius, aided by all the improvements of former ages . . . is to be exerted in planning and executing a form of government which shall [be] . . . the largest empire that ever existed."

In 1823 John Quincy Adams, somewhat more modestly, told a Cabinet meeting that the world must be "familiarized with the idea of considering our proper dominion to be the continent of North America."

The high-water mark in imperialistic public pronounce-
ment came in 1854. With the slavery issue at its height, the
United States considered the possibility of acquiring Cuba,
and Secretary of State James Buchanan instructed the
American Ministers to Spain, France and Britain to make
recommendations. They proposed offering Spain $120 mil-
lion (an astronomical sum in those days) for the island.
They went on: "But if Spain, dead to the voice of her own
interest, and actuated by stubborn pride and a false sense
of honor . . . ." should refuse to sell, what should the
American course be? Predictably, they concluded that
"by every law, human or divine, we shall be justified in
wresting it from her if we possess the power."

Most historians agree with the public figures quoted
above as to our imperialistic tendencies. Indeed, most of
them would agree that the principal difference between
our imperialism and that of other countries has been the
remarkable speed with which our aims were achieved.
And, as usual, this speedy success generated its full quota
of myths.

Louisiana—an ill-defined and enormous territory including much of the Mississippi Valley—was no stranger to
real-estate transactions. Originally settled by the French,
it had gone to Spain in 1762 as part of the reshuffling after
the Seven Years' War. The deal included land west of the
river and the Island of New Orleans, site of the city, which
commanded the river's mouth.

By 1800 Americans had spilled over the Alleghenies and
were anxious to float their goods southward to New
Orleans, which in Spanish hands was a potential obstacle

to such down-river commerce. With a wary eye on these potential troublemakers, Charles IV of Spain was not unwilling to part with this hard-to-defend and difficult-to-administer area. He did so to France in the "secret" but soon-leaked treaty of San Ildefonso in 1800.

Temporarily at peace in Europe, Napoleon Bonaparte turned his attention elsewhere and left Spain in undisturbed possession of Louisiana. Bonaparte proposed to reconquer Santo Domingo (part of the Caribbean island of Hispaniola), where an ex-slave, Toussaint L'Ouverture, had established a republic. Louisiana would provide a granary for the reconquered Santo Domingo. Unfortunately for Bonaparte's ambition, heroic native resistance and mosquito-carried yellow fever cost the French fifty thousand troops without buying reconquest—all of which diminished the importance of Louisiana in the First Consul's eyes.

By the spring of 1802 news of the San Ildefonso treaty had spread to the United States, prompting Jefferson to write Robert Livingston, his Minister to France. Jefferson pointed out that the return of Louisiana to France "completely reverses all the political relations of the United States . . . ." and, he might have added, most of the political principles of Thomas Jefferson. The moment that an active France displaces a passive Spain at the foot of the Mississippi, he proclaimed, "we must marry ourselves to the British fleet and nation. We must turn all our attention to a maritime force. . . ." Finally, without appealing to law or Constitution, he instructed Livingston to offer to buy New Orleans and the Floridas (nothing was said here about Louisiana).

In the autumn Spain revoked American use of the port of New Orleans, making matters even more urgent. Western wrath prompted Jefferson to send James Monroe to supplement Livingston. They were instructed to secure the Island of New Orleans, some land on the east bank of the Mississippi, and all or any part of the Floridas. They were authorized to spend up to $10 million.

By the spring of 1803 the likelihood of new European disturbances had shattered Napoleon's dream of reconquering the Dominican Republic. On April 11, he announced that he had decided to sell all of Louisiana. Thus opened several days of complicated maneuvering which ended with the Americans (authorized to spend $10 million for New Orleans and the Floridas) agreeing to pay $15 million for Louisiana, "the extent of which no man knew."

The treaty by no means ended the pressure on Jefferson. His Federalist opponents, largely prevented by their New England location from sharing in the exploitation of the new areas, claimed executive usurpation and violation of the Constitution, to the strict-constructionist President's acute embarrassment. The protest reached such a point that Jefferson even proposed a constitutional amendment to legalize what he honestly felt to be beyond his power. At, last, however, he discarded his principles and took the necessary steps, setting an example of tailoring principle to practice, and the transaction was complete.

The last Anglo-American territorial dispute concerned Oregon. By a treaty of 1819 it extended north and south between latitude 42° and 54°40′ North, and ran east from the Pacific Ocean to the Rocky Mountains. An earlier agreement (1818) had established the Canadian-American boundary along the 49th parallel as far as the Rockies. It also left the Oregon country, as defined above, open to the subjects of each without prejudice to the claims of either. But as control of the mouth of the Columbia River was essential to Britain's contact with the Canadian interior, she kept the Americans south of the river. Britain had no desire to retain this territory other than for its strategic importance.

A great trek of Missouri Valley farmers along the Oregon Trail followed the panic of 1837; they could neither secure valid title to land for settlement nor cross the Columbia into its rich northern valley. Their protests made Oregon an issue in the campaign of 1844. Candidate James K. Polk's platform declared that "our title to the whole of the Territory of Oregon is clear and unquestionable. . . ." During the campaign his supporters translated this into the picturesque slogan "Fifty-four Forty or Fight."

In January, 1846, Polk confided to his diary that "the only way to treat John Bull [the English] was to look him in the eye. . . ." Since war talk on both sides had followed his inaugural, and since a settlement extending the boundary to the Pacific along the 49th parallel soon followed his diary entry, it was long believed that Polk's "icy stare" had forced a British surrender. The facts, however, are otherwise.

Indeed, it has now been proven that Polk was bluffing, while Lord Aberdeen, the British Foreign Minister, held most of the aces. Aberdeen had concluded that the crucial triangle was not worth a fight, and was willing to settle at the 49th parallel. He had, however, some domestic political problems and could not afford to back down in the face of Polk's belligerence. He handled the matter by telling Louis McLane, Polk's Minister to London, that he would not oppose naval armaments "founded upon the contingency of war with the United States . . . ." and that such would include "the equipment of thirty sails of the line besides steamers and other vessels of war . . . ." This prospect was hardly pleasing to Polk.

It would seem, then, that Aberdeen's stare was icier than Polk's. At any rate, the President backed down and hinted that he would submit to the Senate any British proposal for compromise. Matters then took a complicated path to an agreement extending the boundary, as Aberdeen had long been willing to do, and as Polk was persuaded to do by the British naval threat.

Polk has often been cast as the personification of Manifest Destiny. Texas had been annexed a few days before his inauguration, but Mexico had not yet accepted the unwelcome fact. We have just witnessed Polk's acquisition of Oregon, and the Mexican War (1846–48) will round out the story. This last was long written up as a case of the bully stealing candy from a baby. In fact, the bully was a bit less aggressive and the baby a bit more robust.

It has often been suggested that Polk deliberately sought war with Mexico. In fact, he was relatively patient with Mexican ill-treatment of American citizens and dilly-dallying on payment of well-established commercial and personal claims. He sent John Slidell on a fruitless mission designed to trade these for land. Only on Slidell's return did Polk propose a war message.

Again, the sweeping success of the American army has tended to cast doubts upon Mexican fighting ability. The facts are that differences between the two powers in manpower and military experience were less than a later generation would realize.

Mexicans had been reading history (always a dangerous pastime) and had failed to find much evidence of American military ability in the War of 1812. They doubted whether the North would support a war which might add new slave territory. And they would have the advantage of fighting a defensive war. In view of all this, it is not surprising that Mexico *initiated* military hostilities.

Finally, there has been a shift in the evidence of Polk's supposed territorial ambitions. It is true that the Treaty of Guadalupe Hidalgo relieved Mexico of Texas and all or part of the present states of California, Nevada, Arizona, Utah, New Mexico, Colorado and Wyoming for the bargain price of $15 million cash and the American assumption of claims up to $3,250,000. The sum is really quite reasonable when it is remembered that gold was discovered in California a few days earlier. This would seem to be enough to satisfy any appetite for territory, but there is good evidence that Polk himself opposed a strong and growing sentiment for the annexation of *all* Mexico.

5. The Brothers' War

Secessionists leaving the Union.

Slavery was the most deep-seated cancer ever to afflict American life. Even today it is difficult to view slavery objectively, and historians are still sifting the evidence in search of the truth.

Since slavery was a sectional question, let us remember that myths arose on both sides. Let us remember, too, that it was not originally confined to the South. For complex reasons slavery grew less and less profitable in the North and finally it disappeared. While this was happening, the cotton gin vastly increased Southern production, and so made the institution of slavery more attractive, and finally, it was believed, essential.

Myths of Slavery

At the risk of oversimplification, let us list the charges on both sides of the issue. Slavery, said the Northerners, reduced human beings to the condition of marketable property, and so destroyed the fundamentals of human dignity. It left untold millions to live under subhuman conditions. It violated family ties. It promoted sexual immorality. It led to violence.

The South asserted that slavery was essential: "Cotton *is* King," claimed Senator James H. Hammond. Not only was it King, it was a positive good, both to blacks and whites. Slaves, said the Southerners, were better off than their counterparts in Northern factories. And bitter charges were leveled against Northern abolitionists for interfering in something which was really none of their business.

Emphasizing again the controversial nature of these charges, and remembering that many matters are still under debate, let us try to reduce some of the myths on both sides.

The fact is that Southern claims as to the well-being of slaves were exaggerated. Slave life-style varied widely, as did that of their masters. The more fortunate lived on a level approaching that of their owners. On the whole, however, the slave led a hard and meager existence. He was at the mercy of a master who was driven by a need to produce and was therefore too apt to view his slaves as mere instruments to that end.

Southerners loudly and repeatedly claimed that the slave's lot was preferable to that of the "wage slave" in a Northern factory, subjected to conditions far less tolerable than that of their own "servants." They had a point, as factory conditions were miserable. It would be fair to say that actual conditions were equally bad, but that the slave's lack of freedom makes Southern protests sound fairly hollow.

The Southern belief that slavery was a positive good could hardly be supported in the areas of family relationships or sexual morality. Family inheritances and financial crises forced the sale of slaves—dividing wives from husbands and children from their parents. Families were often permanently separated; this practice raised Northern charges of inhumanity. Again, Southern claims of similar separations in white society, for business or military reasons, seem weak.

The superior/inferior relationship between master and female slave hardly led to respect for female chastity. Many masters begot half-breed children who never left the plantation, thus adding to the labor supply. Slaves could also be sold "down the river" for prices depending upon the broadness of their backs (for field hands) and the shapeliness of their bodies (for young and light-skinned women). It thus requires a good deal of imagination to accept the argument that slavery promoted Southern morality.

The master/slave relationship also increased the likelihood of physical brutality. Southerners were quick to deny Northern charges of such excess, but the fact remains that individual slaves were horribly mistreated. Though slave uprisings were difficult to engineer and almost always ineffective, enough of them did occur to cast doubt on the Southern claim of humane treatment.

All in all, the Southern defense against Northern objections to the slave system fails to stand up to examination. Now let us look at the record from the Southern side.

One of the most widely accepted Southern beliefs was the myth of King Cotton. Almost everyone believed that cotton was absolutely essential to a successful Southern economy, and therefore that slavery was equally essential. Unfortunately, this was never put to the test before the Civil War because cotton culture was so profitable, but there is plenty of evidence that many different kinds of crops could be, and later were, planted successfully in the South.

The myth of King Cotton was also an important factor in the Southern defeat. It was widely assumed that Southern cotton was a necessity for the English textile mills. It was hoped that the need to keep the mills running would force the British to aid the Confederacy. Several factors belied this hope. For one thing, extra-large Southern crops had filled British warehouses to overflowing. When these crops became depleted, supplies began arriving from Egypt and India.

Also, the English mill-hands spoke out against recognition, and many of them found alternative employment. At the same time, there were crop shortages in England which the North could ease through increased production, aided by the newly developed McCormick reaper. Why, then, should Britain recognize a slavery-defending South?

Contrary to the Southern myth, not all Northerners were abolitionists. Many were too busy or too indifferent to take up moral causes. Few Northern mill-owners, for example, were loud supporters of abolition.

Even if the North had supported abolition unanimously, the likelihood of harmonizing the various approaches was slight. There were many different humanitarian attacks on slavery, which the South lumped together under a single umbrella called "abolitionism." In fact, abolitionist attitudes varied widely. The Free-Soilers were not abolitionists at all; they simply opposed extension of slavery into the areas acquired by mid-century expansionism. Even the true abolitionists differed sharply over their goals: immediate emancipation, with or without compensation to the masters; emancipation with compensation to the slaves themselves; emancipation with deportation to Africa; and finally, abolition by force of arms—a course advocated only by extremists.

Myths of Secession

In the 1850s slavery was an issue in a succession of episodes. The Kansas-Nebraska Act of 1854, by repealing
the Missouri Compromise, opened the two territories to
slavery and reopened barely healed sectional wounds.
Three years later the Supreme Court's Dred Scott decision made it impossible to exclude slavery from any territory prior to statehood. The Lincoln-Douglas Debates of
1858 were in themselves a standoff, but kept the issue
alive. In 1860 the new Republican Party's candidate, Abraham Lincoln, was elected President, receiving only 40 percent of the popular vote.

Slavery was a large issue in the campaign, and Lincoln's
position became of great importance to both sides. South
Carolina took Lincoln's election as enough of a danger to
justify secession, and did so in December, 1860, before
Lincoln was even inaugurated. Mississippi, Florida, Ala-
bama, Georgia, Louisiana and Texas followed shortly
thereafter (Virginia, Arkansas, Tennessee, and North
Carolina went out later).

It has been argued that Lincoln's election was not an
immediate threat to slavery. The war which ended that
institution failed to establish this, but the weight of evidence seems to indicate that Lincoln's hostility to slavery
was close to being mythical.

One undoubted myth is the charge that the war grew out
of factors other than slavery. In the early stages of the post-

war period Jefferson Davis and Alexander Stevens argued that Southern constitutional rights had been sufficiently violated to justify secession and war. The argument that the highly protectionist Morrill Act frightened the agricultural South into war loses some force when we remember that seven states had seceded prior to its final passage in 1861.

Northern writers have for years concentrated upon slavery as a cause. The most vigorous attack upon this interpretation was made by Charles A. Beard, this time accompanied by his wife, Mary. Their jointly-written *The Rise of American Civilization* (1927) argued that war came from the desire of Northern industrialism to dominate Southern agrarianism. They became the leaders of a revisionist school which for some years sought to push slavery into the background. Then, in 1950, Professor Allan Nevins swung the pendulum back toward the original view, that slavery was the prime cause—among others—and there the matter rests to date.

The Civil War

Between the attack on Fort Sumter and Robert E. Lee's surrender at Appomattox Court House, the Civil War ran its bloody course. Much ink has been spilled in listing the reasons why Northern victory was inevitable, or factors suggesting Southern superiority and possible victory. Prominent among the latter is Lee, around whom an aura of greatness has grown.

It is now coming to be accepted that Lee, although a

superb strategist in a limited area, had little training or experience on the broader front. For example, his main theater of operations was Virginia, and he served only a few weeks as Commander-in-Chief of all the Confederate armies. Again, he seems to have been primarily a textbook soldier, looking at war as a game to be played according to fairly rigid rules. The Civil War introduced a good many variations on the old routine, such as trench warfare, the rifled cannon, wire entanglements, and observation balloons. Lee's opponents seem to have adjusted to these new tactics more flexibly than he. And finally, his preoccupation with the technical side seems to have left him less alert than his opposition to the clear relationship between the military and the political aspects of war.

Historically wars have been planned by high commands, and fought by common soldiers. It has been argued that the Southern foot soldier was fighting, as had his Revolutionary ancestors, for independence, and that his outdoor life prepared him for battle conditions. It has also been said that until the war's last phase, Lee usually had manpower reasonably comparable to that of his opponents. Why, then, did the Southern armies fail to keep up a successful fight?

Professor David Donald has suggested a possible explanation which is worth thinking about: because of his strong belief in democracy, the Southern soldier found it impossible to submit, over the long run, to the discipline necessary for the creation of a successful army. In Donald's own words, he "made an admirable fighter but a poor soldier."

Of course, a leader's success or failure depends in considerable part on the opposition which he has to face. After a slow start, Abraham Lincoln emerged with a clear conception of grand strategy and of the essential politico-military relationship which Lee never attained. Moreover, after a period of military reverses, Ulysses S. Grant came out of the West to put Lincoln's grand strategy on the map. The two worked in harmony throughout the remainder of the war, exerting on a wide front the extra pressure made possible by a superior economy in order to wear down the enemy. The South, too, seems never to have developed other commanders of Lee's caliber, or men comparable to Grant's subordinates on the other side.

The Myth of "The Great Emancipator"

One of the most firmly fixed and least accurate of American myths is that of Abraham Lincoln, the Great Emancipator, "striking the shackles from four million slaves." As a matter of fact, Lincoln's behavior in this area had to be exceedingly delicate, since any hasty action might alienate one or more of five border slave states to the point of secession. He was therefore compelled to soft-pedal slavery at first and to wage his war on the issue of preserving the Union. It was only when the border states were reasonably secure that he dared issue (in September, 1862) a preliminary Emancipation Proclamation that unless the seceding states returned to the Union by January, 1863, all their slaves would be free.

The war, of course, continued, and on January 1 he made the Proclamation final—as final, that is, as a stroke of the pen could make it in the eleven states over which his control was still very much in doubt. Also, the Proclamation did nothing whatever for the slaves in the border states. It was only later, by the Thirteenth Amendment to the Constitution (1865), that Congress actually freed all the slaves.

The Myth of Reconstruction

A decade of brutality and corruption, forced upon the South by Northern Radicals and their Southern collaborators—this is the broad picture of Reconstruction which has been accepted for generations.

The bare facts of Reconstruction are as follows. Andrew Johnson, a staunch Democrat, became President in 1865 after being placed on the Lincoln ticket to attract his fellow party members to the Republican camp. Once in office, his approach to Reconstruction became a lenient one, resembling Lincoln's in principle though differing in detail.

By December, 1865, he had recognized new governments in ten of the eleven seceding states which had accepted his relatively modest requirement that they renounce secession and recognize abolition. Presently, as a result of an election in 1866, control of Congress passed into the hands of the "Radical" Republicans. They repudiated the Johnson formula and refused to seat the Southern Congressmen chosen according to it. They also set up a new hurdle for readmission—acceptance of the Fourteenth Amendment to the Constitution, conferring citizenship on the freedmen.

With Presidential encouragement, the Southern states except Tennessee rejected the Amendment. The Radicals, firmly in the saddle and incensed both at their own President and their former enemies, responded by subjecting the South to military rule from 1867 to 1877. They rewarded Southern rejection of the Fourteenth Amendment by adding a Fifteenth, conferring the ballot on Blacks, and making ratification of both Amendments a condition of reentry into the Union, a process completed only in 1877.

In interpreting this period, Professor William A. Dunning's *Reconstruction, Political and Economic, 1865–1877* sketched the first broad outlines in 1909, and his students filled in the blanks over the next couple of decades. In 1929 Claude G. Bowers, a journalist masquerading as a historian, used his skills to add colorful detail.

According to Dunning and Bowers, the South became a stage across which paraded thousands of unsavory characters who inflicted a succession of evils upon that unhappy section. Encouraged by the all-powerful Congressional Radicals, a horde of "carpetbaggers" (Northerners) descended upon the hapless South. These enlisted the "scalawags" (Southerners willing to profit at the expense of their neighbors and friends) in their unholy schemes. The newly freed slaves fell easy prey to their joint manipulations, and the result was an era of unparalleled corruption, inefficiency, and brutality in which, in Bowers' words, the Southern people "literally were put to the torture." The mass of Southern whites revolted against this as soon as the military occupation was ended in 1877. Dunning and Bowers' highly biased approach came, unhappily, to in-

spire the bulk of historical writing on the period until the
1930s.

It should be clear by now that historians like to revise
one another's findings. Often, this is important for historical accuracy. For example, the history of a President's
foreign policy, written while he is in office or shortly after
his term has ended, may have to be drastically revised
when, years later, his personal papers and the diplomatic
archives of his own and other governments are opened to
scholars. Again, one group of writers may stress the social
and political aspects of a period, neglecting the economic
side; this needs correction and the scholar who does so
renders a service. Fortunately, this kind of revisionism has
appeared in the more recent books on Reconstruction.

First, it would appear that the Radicals were neither as
all-powerful nor as unpleasant as we were once asked to
believe. It is true that their programs enforced severe policies upon the South. It is also true that they were only able
to enact these programs with the aid of non-Radical votes.
Therefore, if Reconstruction had a vindictive side, all the
blame for it cannot be laid on the Radicals' doorstep.

Again, though the immediate effects of their programs
were harsh, a strong measure of idealism inspired many of
their leaders. The Fourteenth and Fifteenth Amendments,
designed to improve the lot of black people and to integrate
them into the fabric of Southern democracy, testify to this
idealism. The fact that the South nullified the effects of
these amendments for generations after Reconstruction
cannot obscure their intent.

And finally, there has been a moderation of some of the
charges of brutality used in the older accounts. Remember,

too, that the South had tried to break up the Union. It may come as a surprise that few of her leaders were arrested; still fewer were imprisoned; none were tried for the treason with which they might reasonably have been charged; and only one paid with his life for allegedly mistreating Union prisoners. Indeed, before long, ex-Confederate leaders were back in the current of state and national politics.

What, then, shall we say of Reconstruction? First, that it was an inevitable aftermath of a crisis so long maturing and so bitterly resolved on the battlefield. Second, that Reconstruction was carried out with less finesse and more bitterness than we today might wish, but with more of the former and less of the latter than was long held to be the case. And, finally, that the failures and bitterness of Reconstruction have perpetuated themselves far too long, creating sectional antagonisms which still, unfortunately, persist.

6. A Different Nation Emerges

THE SPANISH BRUTE ADDS MUTILATION
TO MURDER

The jingo press calls for war with Spain.

While the wounds of war were still healing, the country entered a period of domestic business. In the 1870s, the farmer, the miner, and the rancher were moving west; first by oxcart and wagon train, then by the Wells Fargo Express, and finally on shiny steel rails. Towns quickly followed the early settlers, buying their produce and supplying their needs. In the East, immigrants swelled the slums of cities, and new industries thrived, making goods for East and West alike. A railroad network moved goods and produce back and forth across the country.

During this period some businessmen and industrialists amassed huge fortunes and sought, often successfully, to control not only their own business and industrial empires but others as well. According to long-established legend, these tycoons were so arrogant and greedy as to earn the name of "robber barons."

The Myth of the Robber Barons

When American business began to burst its seams in the post-Reconstruction period, some American industrialists who were in strategic positions rose to great wealth and power. A series of writers found the analogy to the feudal robber barons too good to miss and transferred the term from medieval to modern literature. The term appears in print as early as 1869, and gained new approval in Henry Demarest Lloyd's *Wealth against Commonwealth* (1894).

Its most popular and spiteful treatment is in Matthew Josephson's *The Robber Barons* (1934), from which a few sample characterizations will be drawn.

The "same combination of ruthlessness and optimism" that inspired "the socialist statesmen of modern Russia" enabled Andrew Carnegie to reach the top in the manufacture of steel, in great demand for railroad and other construction. A "conjunction of favorable circumstance[s]" gave him "crushing advantages over rivals in the field. Such advantages the rising barons of heavy industry pursued with as sure a scent as did the quarreling princes of olden times. . . ." John D. Rockefeller moved from produce into oil, where his "ruthless economies" contributed to success in the "merciless and unprincipled competition of rivals and his own unpitying logic and coldly resolute methods were doubtless the consequences of the brutal free-for-all from which he emerged with certain crushing advantages." His "instinct for conspiracy" contributed to securing secret "rebates" or kickbacks on railroad shipments of his oil which helped him outdistance and eventually destroy many competitors.

Such monumental operations took money. Banks had traditionally supplied this commodity and here the figure of J. Pierpont Morgan loomed large. In a period of transition when "the rule of money-lender or 'financier' was to supplant that of the 'manufacturer' or the undertaker of business projects . . . ." Morgan and his lieutenants set up a system of interlocking railroad directorates, by which he obtained "virtually absolute control of twelve great systems."

The point need not be labored further. Josephson, the

most vivid among many portrayers of the robber baron, painted Morgan as a ruthless destroyer of competition, a fortune hunter on an unprecedented scale and, generally, a reasonably unsavory character. This harsh portrait of the robber baron has been softened by time and by greater knowledge.

The term "Gay Nineties" is a myth, particularly when applied to the common man. Between 1889–93, eleven thousand Kansas farm mortgages were foreclosed; and by 1900, loan companies owned 90 percent of the state's land. During this decade, the national average of workers' wages dropped from $438 to $428 per year. In that same period, 160,329 companies went bankrupt. If the farmer could afford a newspaper during this period, he might read of Cornelius Vanderbilt's million-dollar home or of Jay Gould's half-million-dollar yacht.

Whether or not he read of these signs of affluence, the farmer had to pay what he considered exorbitant railroad rates to get his grain to market. The federal government, too, had given the railroads huge land grants, often to a depth of several miles on either side of their right of way, in order to stimulate construction. These areas were salable, and the farmer believed this government practice lined the pockets of the businessman with ill-deserved wealth. The railroads and their directors were immediately distrusted. The farmers carried their distrust to such an extent that it was eventually projected into politics through the Populist movement.

Nowadays, new evidence tends to soften this portrait somewhat. It seems clear that most of the railroad fortunes were made either in speculation or manipulation, rather than by gouging the farmer. No matter how loudly he protested about high freight rates, statistics show that from 1870–1900 the curve of such rates was almost always downward. Although the farmer charged the government with undue generosity in its land-donation policy, it now seems apparent that the railroads often forfeited much of their land by failing to lay track. Moreover, the building of railroads increased the value of the nearby land, still held by the government or the farmer, so that the wealth was not distributed too unevenly.

The robber barons were men of their own time. No amount of whitewash will disguise all the stains of their sharp financial practices, their misuse of the labor force, their rigging of the market to increase the value of their securities and so fatten their own bank balances, or their cutthroat competition which often injured the public as well as the losers. However, if we carefully examine the present structure and activities of big business, we may find that the robber baron concept has not entirely disappeared. This does not excuse the men of the '70s, '80s, and '90s, but it does put them in the proper perspective.

It must be kept in mind that not all businessmen were destructive to all interests save their own. Whatever W. H. Vanderbilt may have meant by his famous statement, "The public be damned," not all of his fellow tycoons adopted this attitude. Many of them benefited the economic climate of their own day, and some became public benefactors on a huge scale. It is impossible at this point to know how much of their philanthropy stemmed from guilty consciences and how much from an honest concern for succeeding generations, but whatever the motivation, the results have been impressive.

Let us look briefly at a few of the benefits. Carnegie,

for example, made millions from steel, but the track he produced helped to span a continent. Hill amassed his railroad millions while providing the means of opening the West to agricultural and industrial production.

When we look at benefits extending beyond the donors' lifetimes, the list is formidable. Carnegie and Rockefeller gave their names to foundations. Carnegie Tech and Stanford and Vanderbilt Universities will outlast the fame of their football teams. Rockefeller did not actually give his name to a university, but in the 1920s the University of Chicago's official letterhead still bore the modest subscript: "Founded by John D. Rockefeller." Carnegie's gifts to the public library movement were generous.

How shall we look at the tycoons of the past? Perhaps by remembering their constructive contributions, but not letting these blind us to their sometimes disruptive rivalries or their often devious practices.

The Spanish-American War

While the domestic difficulties were sorting themselves out, the nation suddenly jumped its continental borders in a burst of overseas imperialism. The destruction of the second-class battleship *Maine* in Havana harbor triggered what Secretary of State John Hay was to call a "splendid little war." Lasting from April 21 to August 12, 1898, its conclusion found Spain completely and humiliatingly defeated, Cuba nominally free, and the United States, somewhat to its own surprise, in possession of the Philippine and Hawaiian Islands, Puerto Rico, and Guam, with a Samoan outpost at Pago-Pago shortly thereafter.

Contrary to most accounts, this spilling over continental borders was not the birth of American imperialism. It was merely the continuation of an expansionist trend which has characterized this country's foreign policy almost from the very beginning.

Years of hostility and repression had marked Spain's relations with her Cuban colony. Americans could hardly ignore such unpleasantness so close to home. When William McKinley entered the White House, he approached the facts of Spanish oppression with his customary deliberateness. For months he withstood considerable pressures to use force of arms to right Cuba's wrongs.

Some of these pressures were exerted by a sensationalist press, led by William Randolph Hearst and Joseph Pulitzer. Engaged in a battle for newspaper circulation in New York City, Hearst's *Journal* and Pulitzer's *World* tried to outdo each other in publishing stories of atrocities in Cuba and in damning McKinley's passivity. The influence of the press in actually starting the war cannot be determined but it can safely be said that few newspapers were as vocal as the *Journal* and the *World*, and that many actually opposed the venture.

McKinley was more likely to listen to the voice of big business, whose interest he esteemed highly. Here the evidence is conflicting. Professor Julius W. Pratt has argued that the business community feared war's adverse effects on its $100 million of annual trade with Cuba and its investments of half that amount in the island. In a later book, Professor Walter LaFeber found that many tycoons supported the war. As in the case of press influence, it is difficult to achieve an accurate balance between conflicting claims.

Clearly there were many pressures on the President. It has at least been hinted that he resisted them. What, then, of the charge that McKinley made war inevitable after Spain had accepted his conditions for peace, prepared and offered on March 27, 1898? The facts are these.

A private letter from Spain's able Ambassador in Washington, Dupuy de Lôme, commented unfavorably on McKinley's annual message to Congress. This found its way, by devious channels, to Mr. Hearst and from there into print. De Lôme had the bad luck of having his private opinion (to which he had a perfect right) aired in the *Journal*. The episode led to de Lôme's prompt resignation and a great public furor, although American journalists were themselves being much more unpleasant to their own President.

Less than a week later, on February 15, 1898, the *Maine*, quietly at anchor in Havana harbor, blew up, bringing death to over 250 Americans and new bitterness to Spanish-American relations. The numerous investigations of the tragedy were all conducted by one or the other of the nations involved, and there has never been a definitive answer to the question of responsibility. The immediate charge of official Spanish involvement now seems ridiculous, as Spain was desperately trying to avoid a war, not to start one. The explosion immediately gave the jingo press new ammunition with which to attack both Spain and the President.

And where was McKinley? He was preparing his proposal for peace, mentioned above. The proposal was three-fold: (1) an early armistice to end the fighting between Spain and the rebels; (2) an end to the harsh policy of imprisoning rebels in concentration camps; and (3) a suggestion that unless peace had been achieved by October 1, McKinley himself should "be the final arbiter between Spain and the insurgents"—a thinly-veiled demand that the President of the United States have the power to end Spain's possession of Cuba.

McKinley was also reading the newspaper attacks on his failure to respond to such provocation as the de Lôme affair and the *Maine*. But he was also mindful of the power of a group of conservative Senators opposed to violent measures, and he heard from his Consul in Havana of the danger of hostilities to Americans in Cuba. Under these confused and conflicting circumstances, McKinley stalled for time. He wrote a war message, showed it to members of both Houses, and locked it up, as he said, until there was no longer any danger to "a single American life" in Cuba.

Spain's reply to McKinley's peace proposal was delayed until April 9. It hedged its acceptance of the armistice and ignored McKinley's third demand completely. This left the President up a high stump. Congressional radicals were by this time demanding recognition of the Cuban insurgents; conservatives had advanced a demand for the annexation of the island; and the jingo press was demanding that Spain be taught a lesson.

Still trying for delay, McKinley took his war message out of the safe and asked Congress (on April 11) for "authority to use the armed forces" to "secure a full and final termination of hostilities . . . ." in Cuba. Only on April 19 was he presented with a resolution authorizing war. His options for delay at an end, he signed, taking his country into "a war that he did not want for a cause in which he did not believe." Here, be it noted, is no story of warmongering.

The war's military aspects leave little room for myth. Victory followed victory with monotonous regularity. Commodore George Dewey destroyed the Spanish fleet in Manila Bay. A like fate befell Spanish ships at Santiago, Cuba, though American naval marksmanship left something to be desired—over 9,000 shots seem to have registered fewer than 125 hits.

As we have seen, myths tend to attach themselves to colorful individuals. A persistent myth credits Theodore Roosevelt, quite incorrectly, with responsibility for acquiring the Philippines. The story goes that while his superior officer was taking a needed half-day's rest, Assistant Secretary of the Navy Roosevelt, together with his friend Henry Cabot Lodge, cabled orders to Commodore Dewey that in case of war his duty "will be . . . offensive operations in Philippine Islands. . . ." Presumably the victory at Manila followed upon this order, dropping the Philippines into the lap of a surprised McKinley, who, as one writer put it, "with hundreds of thousands of his fellow citizens, proceeded to look up the exact location of the Philippines on the map." What are the facts?

The plan for attacking the Philippines was developed in the Navy Department before Roosevelt was even connected with it. It originated as an exercise in contingency planning, a routine part of naval training. The plan itself was not self-starting, however, and Roosevelt's cable to Dewey only told the latter to be ready in case of need.

McKinley's alleged surprise at receiving the Philippines was as unreal as Roosevelt's role in delivering it. McKinley was well aware of the plan to attack Manila, had repeatedly discussed it with the Secretary of the Navy, and gave his personal approval for the order to attack. Under these circumstances, it would seem highly unlikely that he was unaware of the islands' location.

One last wartime myth may be noted briefly. It centers around the controversy which arose after military success had given McKinley the option of annexing the Philippine Islands. Confronted with this problem, he allegedly told a delegation of Methodist ministers that he sought, and received, divine guidance to an affirmative decision. As he was quoted by one of his hearers, "I am not ashamed to tell you, gentlemen, that I went down on my knees and prayed Almighty God for light and guidance. . . . And one night late it came to me . . . that there was nothing left for us to do but to take them all, and . . . do the very best we could by them, as our fellow men for whom Christ also died. And then I went to bed and went to sleep, and slept soundly."

The long quotation, from which the above is an excerpt, did not appear in print until four years after the event, and has received no support from any other source. Moreover, the author of the reminiscence containing the quotation, an elderly Civil War veteran, had published another book in which he had Abraham Lincoln addressing the Almighty in remarkably similar language in connection with the Battle of Gettysburg.

There was, in fact, no need to invoke Heaven's aid in

supporting the idea of annexation. Large sectors of the American public, at first surprised at the Philippine developments, adjusted with remarkable ease to the idea of overseas possessions. McKinley himself felt this shift clearly enough, and went along with it.

7. Two World Wars

THE SANDWICH MAN

*Ambivalent policies preceded American entry
into World War I.*

The interwar years featured the further development of the imperialism of 1898 in the Philippines and the Caribbean; they witnessed important domestic developments in the area of business and financial regulation; and they saw an ideological split in the Republican party which enabled Woodrow Wilson to defeat William Howard Taft in 1912, bringing with him a Democratic Congress.

A scholar turned politician (he had been a professor, later President, at Princeton, and Governor of New Jersey), Wilson was effective with the written word and, although an able politician, was fairly aloof in most of his personal relationships. He embarked promptly on a program of domestic regulatory legislation which was punctuated by the outbreak of war in Europe in 1914.

The Myth of Neutrality

A standing policy, born of long and often bitter experience, produced an automatic declaration of "neutrality" or impartiality in the European war, designed to avoid American involvement. This became increasingly difficult, and ultimately impossible, to maintain.

Both England and Germany violated our neutrality— the British by a blockade designed to prevent Americans from trading with their enemies; the Germans by an increasingly rigorous submarine campaign aimed at keeping us from trading with the Allies.

The submarine warfare gradually passed from a stage of

inconvenience into one of outrage. Early in 1917 a desperate Germany proclaimed "unrestricted submarine warfare" against all shipping, enemy or neutral, in specified zones. Germany was resigned to war with the United States as a result, but gambled on defeating Britain before American military potential could become effective. Within a few weeks, the subs sank unarmed American ships, with considerable loss of life, and Congress granted Wilson's request for a declaration of war.

A number of myths have arisen in connection with America's entry into the war. First of all, it was not "Woodrow Wilson's War." Though personally pro-Ally, he for months walked a tightrope between annoying but successful British restrictions on American trade with Germany and less successful but more annoying German efforts to limit our trade with the Allies.

Also, Wilson did not "go to war" against Germany. Constitutionally only Congress can declare war, and on April 2, 1917, he could only *ask* that body to exercise that power, which it did four days later by overwhelming majorities of both Houses.

Again, it is highly improbable that the United States went to war because of propaganda from either side, though both Britain and Germany made massive efforts in this area. It is a mistake to believe that the German case was not given proper circulation. It was ultimately ineffective, however, due in large part to the submarine warfare. Both propaganda efforts were influential, the German effort being important earlier and the Allied one later on, but their total impact was not decisive.

A final myth, which was popular in the 1930s, claimed

that our bankers and munitions-makers pressured the government into war to protect their huge loans to the Allies, covering enormous sales of munitions. According to this explanation, our nation was in deep depression in 1914. The war trade and its consequent loans brought us out of this depression, and a government daring to go against this economic bonanza would have been in deep trouble. Evidence, however, is lacking to prove that either bankers or armaments-makers exterted effective pressure. Indeed, on a very practical level, it may be asked why either bankers or armaments-makers would want to destroy the certainty of current profits by seeking the national disaster of war.

Wars are great breeders of myths. Some are born of day-to-day needs to justify and win the struggle; some of later need to minimize its less pleasant aspects. A need for a popular slogan, combined with Wilson's ability with words, produced one such myth, to the effect that we waged a war to "make the world safe for democracy." If the preceding story has not been too greatly condensed, it should be apparent that the submarine, not high principle, triggered the conflict and that its fundamental cause was revulsion against German violation of American rights, rather than any crusade for democracy.

The League of Nations

German acceptance of an armistice on November 11, 1918, cast Wilson in the role of peacemaker. Here his efforts would be frustrated by Republican opposition to the Versailles Treaty, including the Covenant of the League of

Nations, which he brought back from long negotiations at Paris, and which was defeated in the Senate.

Politics, of course, played a part in this defeat. It has been charged, erroneously, that the emergence of "politics" at this point was a new phenomenon, the united war effort having buried such crass matters. Nothing could be further from the truth, for the Republican opposition, skillfully led and more unified than the Democratic majority, had kept a running attack on every phase of the war program.

Forced into a bitter Congressional campaign in 1916, Wilson condemned alleged Republican interference with the war effort and demanded that the voters return a Democratic Congress. They chose Republican majorities in both Houses. Thus ended the myth of a nonpartisan conduct of the war. One can only wonder what influence all this had on the fate of Wilson's treaty.

Many accounts have pictured Wilson at Paris as a lamb among the wolves, walking naively with his head in the clouds and selling his soul for his private invention, the League of Nations. They have pictured him on his return home as a completely rigid advocate of "his" League, to such an extent that he prevented any compromise with the Senate. Again, the facts belie the myths.

Though not an old-timer at international negotiation, Wilson was less of an amateur in diplomacy than his detractors have charged. Academic life offers plenty of opportunities for exercising such talents; so do state and national office, and the conduct of joint wartime operations. He took with him to Paris, then, negotiating ability and a basic nationalism which carried him a long way in dealing with his opposite numbers whose nationalistic ambitions were more selfishly pursued than his own.

Again, the League of Nations was not Woodrow Wilson's brainchild—schemes of international order go back to medieval times. True, he adopted it and pushed its acceptance by the Conference, which showed neither great enthusiasm nor great antipathy toward it. Probably his most fateful contribution was his insistence that it be a basic part of the treaty of peace, whereas his European colleagues preferred it as an afterthought.

All in all, Wilson succeeded rather well in securing his own objectives and in moderating the demands of the other victors. Indeed, the treaty which he brought home can now be seen to have numerous strong points. The fact, however, that it failed to maintain a permanent peace, in large part because of American failure to underwrite it, has dimmed its virtues. The reputation of Wilson as its chief architect has been tarnished.

Once back home, the Senate became Wilson's problem. The Covenant of the League of Nations, which Wilson had attached to the treaty, contained a blanket commitment to American containment of aggression anywhere in the world. Many Senators honestly felt that this, and other parts of the treaty, carried matters too far. Republican opponents sought to safeguard American rights by attaching limiting "reservations" to the treaty. This could be done by a bare majority, whereas a resolution to ratify the treaty required two thirds.

Wilson's problem was whether or not to compromise. He eventually decided against doing so, causing the defeat of the treaty. This also ended all chance of adopting somewhat similar but milder Democratic reservations which might well have commanded enough votes to secure Senate support of the treaty.

However, it must be pointed out that a period of willingness to compromise preceded the rigidity which brought Wilson and his treaty to defeat. After his return from Paris, he made a "very serious effort" to convert Republican Senators. He made it clear that, although he "preferred to have the treaty passed as submitted . . . he was prepared to accept interpretive reservations . . . in a form that did not require its renegotiation."

These efforts to secure moderate Republican support continued through the summer and included meeting with the Senate Committee on Foreign Relations. An impasse brought him to the belief that compromise on suitable terms was unobtainable.

Wilson then decided to tour the country in the fall of 1919 in defense of an unamended Treaty. In the course of this he suffered a "massive stroke which paralyzed the right side of his body and affected his vision and sensation on that side." The point here is that he was less adamant in his opposition than most history books would have us believe.

A Between-Wars Myth

One of the sturdiest myths of the interwar years was that our unhappy experience in World War I left the United States so intent on domestic concerns as to create a mood of complete withdrawal from the outside world. It is true that national concerns were, as always, of great importance. The 1920s saw a productive economy reach one of its highest peaks of prosperity. This in turn generated a speculative mania, climaxing in 1929 in the stock-market crash and the Great Depression.

Preoccupation with "boom and bust," however, should not obscure the true picture of American international attitudes in the 1920s. We were heavily involved in international affairs, too numerous to chronicle here—in Europe, in Latin America, and in the Far East. However, one hangover from World War I remained: never did we permit involvement, no matter how intimate, to lead to commitment to all-out cooperation in solving world problems.

Pearl Harbor

In the 1930s Adolf Hitler's Nazis were rearming Germany. First, they reoccupied the German Rhineland. In 1938 they swallowed Austria and nibbled at Czechoslovakia, annexing it formally in 1939. Meantime, Benito Mussolini's fascist Italians seized Ethiopia in an attempt to revive the grandeur that had once characterized the Roman Empire. Finally, Hitler loosed his troops on Poland, and World War II was on.

In the East, successive Japanese aggressions in the 1930s against Manchuria and later against China proper caused mixed American reactions. Continued hostilities injured our long-time Chinese friends. On the other hand, economic relations with Japan were close and lucrative.

The fall of France stimulated Japanese military activity in French Indochina, in an effort to secure needed raw materials, including petroleum. Fearing a threat to the Philippines, President Franklin Roosevelt set a partial embargo on the sale of war matériel to Japan. When this proved ineffective, he froze Japanese assets in the United States and cut off the sale of oil—a dire threat to Japan's reserves, depletion of which would force withdrawal from China. This was a decisive factor in Japan's earnestly-debated decision to attack the American fleet at Pearl Harbor.

Hoping to win a quick victory in Southeast Asia before recovery could bring American potential to bear, Japanese warplanes immobilized six of eight battleships, damaged others, and inflicted some thirty-five hundred casualties. The attack was as surprising as it was successful, and much ink and energy have been spent trying to explain how such a disaster could occur.

American cryptographers had already broken some of the Japanese communications codes, and it was pretty certain that a blow would be struck somewhere on December 7. As early as November 25, Secretary of State Cordell Hull's diary recorded Roosevelt's query as to "how we should maneuver them into the position of firing the first shot without allowing too much danger to ourselves." What, then, could be plainer?

Harry Elmer Barnes, Charles A. Beard, George Morgenstern, and others have repeatedly charged that there was a deliberate presidential plot to provoke a Japanese attack in an effort to obtain Roosevelt's own reelection in 1944 and to cover up the failures of his domestic and foreign policies. As Barnes put it: "In order to perpetuate Roosevelt's political ambitions and his mendacious foreign policy some three thousand American boys were quite needlessly butchered. . . ."

Roosevelt's defenders, however, have the better of the argument, and the charges of "deliberate exposure" must be classed among our myths. This, of course, does not explain our failure to be prepared for the impending attack.

Had we been among the experts evaluating the mountains of information available at the time, we should probably have concluded that the ships moving south along the China coast indicated that the threatened blow was aimed somewhere in Southeast Asia. We might have excused ourselves to some extent by pleading the multiplicity of information, poorly handled and badly sorted, which might have alerted us. A Department of State official, having carefully reviewed the official documents, told Professor Bailey that he "found not even the hint of an imminent attack on Pearl Harbor."

The best brief statement I have seen, by Roberta Wohlstetter, still gives no definite answer to the question of responsibility. "The fact of surprise at Pearl Harbor has never been persuasively explained by accusing the participants, individually or in groups, of conspiracy or negligence or stupidity. What this illustrates is rather the very human tendency to pay attention to the signals that support current expectations about enemy behavior. If no one is listening for signals of an attack against a highly improbable target, then it is very difficult for the signals to be heard."

The Myth of Yalta

No other war had seen such speedy transportation and communication. The result was a "war-by-conference," generating military and political decisions affecting world affairs far into the future. Roosevelt and Winston Churchill met eight times, usually in the utmost secrecy. Joseph Stalin attended two sessions with Roosevelt and Churchill (at Teheran and Yalta) and a third (at Potsdam) after Harry S. Truman became President.

The conference at Yalta was held to coordinate the war effort in Europe and to assure Russia's participation in the Far Eastern war once the European struggle had wound down. The decisions that were made dealt with highly controversial matters—matters so secret that sometimes it was impossible to clothe the formal agreement in forthright language; later it was easy for misunderstandings to occur.

Let us look very briefly at the agreements and then see how a myth emerged. Germany was to be brought to its knees in "unconditional surrender," after which it would be partitioned into occupation zones; a postwar United Nations Organization was accepted; Poland, twice a corridor for German invasions of Russia, would be reestablished under "free elections"; other parts of Eastern Europe would be constituted under "democratic regimes"; and Russia promised to enter the war against Japan once Germany had been defeated. These agreements represented compromises on *both* sides.

How did a myth about Yalta develop? Looking back from a Cold War perspective, historians found photographs picturing a gaunt and haggard President. They recalled that on his return he had apologized to Congress for addressing that body from a chair. And within two months he was dead. When Poland and Eastern Europe became Communist, it was easy to charge that a weakened Roosevelt had "given" Eastern Europe and much of the Far East to the Communists. Medical evidence that the President was not seriously ill during the Conference was not available at the time, though it was made public later. Furthermore, few stopped to think that Churchill, about whose physical stamina there was no doubt, had also signed the Yalta agreements.

Certainly, there had been no question of mental or physical deterioration at the Teheran Conference. There is no question, either, that the discussions at Teheran foreshadowed many of the Yalta agreements. There Stalin promised to enter the Far Eastern war after Germany's defeat. The separation of Germany, Poland's boundaries and government, and establishment of a postwar international organization all received attention at Teheran. These discussions sufficiently resemble the Yalta agreements to prove that the latter were not the fault of Roosevelt's alleged physical incompetence. What then of the Yalta agreements themselves and their "betrayal" of American interests?

Probably the biggest factor in creating the myth of Yalta was the deep American fear of communism, at home as well as abroad. The Cold War, which consumed so much of our national energy during the postwar period, focused suspicion on any action which might have helped to create its tensions.

As far as Eastern Europe is concerned, communism could have been kept out only at a cost greater than either Britain or the United States was prepared to pay. As to Poland, it is true that Yalta's promise of democracy was not lived up to. This is due in part to the loose language of the agreement. The Allies were pledged to a "broadly based" government which would be committed to free elections. This language, deliberately vague in order to secure agreement, made it easy for Russia to conspire to avoid holding such elections. This was a violation of a good agreement, not a failure to make one.

In the Far East, critics point out that Roosevelt unnecessarily brought Russia into the war against Japan only days before the Japanese surrendered. American intelligence reports at Yalta had failed to make clear that Japan was on her last legs; hence it was felt that Russian assistance would be necessary in the final push. It so happened that Japan collapsed quite promptly, and Russian assistance proved unnecessary. Thus Russia bought her way cheaply into the Far East.

We must remember, however, that Stalin did as he had promised at Yalta and withdrew from his occupation of Manchuria, which neither agreement nor Western arms could have prevented him from retaining had he wished to do so. It is hard to see how the United States could have prevented a Communist victory in China.

On the whole, it seems fair to say that the Yalta agreements, as written, resulted from fairly normal negotiations in which each party sought to attain its prime objectives, and in which each compromised somewhat short of this goal. If the agreements failed to stand the test of time, this may be because neither their letter or their spirit were observed. That the President "sold out," however, is a myth.

8. A Cold War and a Hot One

"I DISTINCTLY SAW HIM WAVE AT US."

© 1952 by Herblock in The Washington Post

When Communist revolutionaries seized control of Russia, the relatively democratic and capitalistic nations were faced with what they considered a threat to their safety, if not their very existence. Hitler's onslaught on Russia in 1941 forced Russia and the Allies into a marriage of convenience to fight a common foe. Papering over their fundamental differences, each sacrificed thousands of lives, and the United States (through Lend-Lease) contributed vast amounts of matériel to the success of their common effort.

Every war (so far, at least) is followed by a period of readjustment. In this case, the marriage of convenience turned into a cold war.

The Cold War

Let us look at what might be called the orthodox approach to the origins of the cold war. Within a month of Franklin Roosevelt's death, Stalin evinced his intention of dominating Rumania, and later Bulgaria. Repeated efforts to get him to honor his Yalta commitments failed, and were finally abandoned. By 1948, Stalin had erected a ring of Communist-dominated states as protection against democratic infiltration—attaining varying degrees of Soviet influence in Finland, Poland, Bulgaria, Rumania, Albania, and Czechoslovakia, all accompanied by repeated accusations and rising fears in the West.

A complex of events, including a rising feeling among

Truman's advisers that Russia had violated her Yalta prom-
ises, anger at her aggressions in Eastern Europe, and the
evident weakening of Japan in the Far East (with consequent lessening of dependence upon Russian assistance in
that area), probably persuaded the new and inexperienced
President overhastily (and only temporarily) to suspend
Lend-Lease aid to Russia in May, 1945, before the Far
Eastern War was concluded. Later, Stalin reacted unfavorably to American reluctance to honor what both public
and official opinion considered an exorbitant request for a
six-billion-dollar loan to repair some of the German devas-
tation of Russia. These actions confirmed already rising
Russian hostility to the West.

This hostility manifested itself in a number of ways
throughout 1945–46. There were frictions over German
surrender negotiations, over the occupation of Germany,
and over peace treaties with the minor powers at war on
Germany's side. Russia also refused to accept American
proposals to share atomic energy know-how because sharing was conditional on international control and inspec-
tion, not subject to a Russian veto. These recurring problems led the Truman Administration to adopt a policy of
"patience and firmness" which by 1947 had hardened into
one of "containment."

In February, 1947, Britain gave notice of her inability
to continue aiding Greece against internal Communist in-
fluences. Truman and his advisors decided to get tough,
and in March the President proposed the Truman Doctrine, asking Congress for $200 million in aid for Greece
and Turkey, on the ground that "it *must* be the policy of
the United States to support free peoples who are resisting

attempted subjection by armed minorities or by outside pressures." This of course was designed to combat and contain the influence of undesirable ideologies.

In June, Secretary of State George C. Marshall proposed a more positive campaign against "hunger, poverty, desperation, and chaos." Unlike the negatively oriented Truman Doctrine, the Marshall Plan offered to study any concerted plans which Europe (including Russia) might propose, with a view to seeing whether they merited American financial support. Most European nations leaped at the opportunity, and presently offered a set of multi-billion-dollar proposals, which Congress underwrote. Russia mistakenly viewed this as an attack, refused to join, and prevented its satellites from participating.

At this point in the orthodox story, it may well be said that the cold war was on. It must seem that its origins can be largely laid on Russia's doorstep—its suspicions, its hostility, and its failure to cooperate during a difficult period finally resulted in an open attempt to contain Communist influence.

After 1960, writers representing what came to be called the New Left, or radical, point of view began to be heard in the land. They disagreed wholeheartedly with the consensus view described above. They relied heavily on evidence appearing in the voluminous memoirs and published official documents (remember, very little such material has appeared from the Russian side). Like most historians, the radicals differed among themselves on details. They agreed, however, that the cold war was less a response to Russian aggression than a positive American effort to build a postwar world geared to the needs of an expanding

American capitalist economy which sought to dominate the world. This of course endangered Communist security and so forced a peace-loving Russia into tactics of self-defense.

The radical revisionists have the United States, led by Truman and his then Secretary of State, James F. Byrnes, making a crucial decision in 1946. In the words of one of them, rather than use American industrial power "to promote international reconstruction through an international agency," we chose "to use its capacity as an instrument of power-politics, that is, to establish an American hegemony over the existing international power structure." This would be to the advantage of the American economy, which desired an "open door" for trade, allowing the economy to expand indefinitely into a commanding position in world trade. In the interests of preserving their own national security, the Russian reaction was to resist this attempt at economic domination.

So much for generalities. Let us look now at the radical revisionists' approach to some of the aggravating episodes in Russian-American relations. The radicals view the suspension of Lend-Lease aid not as the over-hasty snap judgment of an inexperienced and poorly advised President, but as a deliberate shock tactic, administered by one well aware of its inevitable consequences. Again, American attempts to moderate Russian dominance over Eastern Europe were an aggressive interference with Russia's legitimate "security requirements." Had we been less insistent here, it is argued, "their domination of Eastern Europe might have been much different from what it turned out to be."

Among the radicals there is a fairly concerted effort to

depict the Russians in the early postwar days as moderate and somewhat tentative in their opposition to the West, while American thinking was hardening into a cold war mentality. One revisionist writes of this period of developing attitudes in terms of the long-time Russian advocacy of " 'socialism in one country' in a rather conservative, nationalistic way; the moderation of the 1945–46 interlude can be viewed as a logical extension of this tradition."

The threat of British withdrawal from Greece afforded Truman a long-awaited opportunity. Instead of using the occasion as a means of remedying a locally explosive situation, the President replied by launching, in the Truman Doctrine, "an ideological crusade against totalitarian regimes . . . perhaps the major document in America's cold war offensive." Back of it, allegedly, was the fear of "the menace of expanding communism to the American economy; it could cut off supplies of raw materials for America and curtail trade, eliminating markets for investment capital and surpluses." And its successor, the Marshall Plan, was a reaction to Russia's moves into Eastern Europe. Thus, by mid-1947, the issue had been joined, and the United States was revealed as overtly hostile to Russia's legitimate interests. A long-lasting cold war was on.

Allowing for the exaggerations sometimes resulting from such highly condensed accounts, there is obviously not enough room for both these estimates of Russian-American relations in the early postwar years. Which is reality and which is myth—consensus, or New Left?

It was suggested earlier that successive generations of

historians, "interpreting" and "reinterpreting" history, revise one another, and that this process may in time approach a true picture of the past. While some of the New Left claims may yet find their way to general acceptance, it is this author's judgment that the radical writers have taken too long a step, one which brings them at least to the borderline of mythology. As matters now stand, the revisionists are subject to criticism on two counts: the manner of their scholarship and the validity of their conclusions.

Historians have traditionally maintained that a scholar must weigh the evidence he examines as impartially as he is able, and that he must never tamper with the sources as he finds them. Unfortunately, the revisionists start from the assumption that the Communists were only interested in their own national security, something to which all nations rightly aspire. On the other hand, their approach generally finds American aims self-serving and aggressive.

A recent examination of the work of several (but not all) of the radical revisionists indicates clearly that they have omitted evidence unfavorable to their own point of view while twisting the significance of the facts which they do present correctly. These historians have sometimes been careless about factual accuracy and have taken accurate quotations out of context to support their arguments. While such misuse of the mechanics of scholarship does not necessarily invalidate their conclusions, it should suggest that a reader view this literature with some skepticism.

What can be said of the radical revisionists? The orthodox historians have correctly noted that since 1917 Russia has been obviously bent on spreading its Marxist ideology in any open market. World War II gave no evidence that this generous trait had been abandoned, or that a postwar confrontation could be avoided. On the other hand, the radicals have vigorously and properly emphasized the powerful position of American capitalism at the end of the war. However, their emphasis to date is more on assertion than fact, and a verdict of "not proven" seems in order.

Again, the radicals' heavy emphasis on economic determinism may be questioned on the ground that it ignores other factors influencing policymakers in a democracy. Stalin had no powerful Congress, press, or public opinion to push him toward a given course of action. American policymakers have always had to trim their sails to the public and Congressional breeze. This, in the period from September, 1945, to March, 1946, was blowing hard in favor of a stronger policy.

Also, policy must be determined on the spot, and not on the basis of later historical research. Today, it is generally agreed that Stalin was less bent on peddling communism in a larger market than American policymakers believed. But, in the 1940s, the creation of a ring of East-European satellites looked to Truman and his associates like a prelude to carrying similar tactics into Western Europe.

The Myth of "Peace with Honor"

It is ironic that America's longest period of hostilities was never formally declared a war. The "war that wasn't" was compounded by less-than-frank Presidential actions and less-than-alert Congressional responses. The facts can be stated briefly.

Nineteenth-century French colonialism had established an Indochinese empire including Vietnam, Laos, and Cambodia; and France elected to retain Indochina after World War II. Communism, combined with a rising sense of nationalism in northern Vietnam, led to all-out war by the end of 1946. This war went steadily against the French, to the great concern of the United States. Worried that a combination of Russian and Chinese communism (fortified by a thirty-year mutual defense treaty in 1950) might lead to world-wide Communist aggression, successive American administrations made ever-increasing economic and non-combatant military assistance to France's deteriorating war effort.

In October of 1954, President Dwight Eisenhower made a somewhat vague promise of "aid" to South Vietnam, contingent upon internal "reforms" by a government which never made them. By a somewhat mysterious process, this promise was translated by the mid-1960s into billions of dollars of economic aid and active military combat assistance in which American troops sustained casualties of forty-five thousand dead and two hundred thousand wounded.

Those who did not live through this period may find it difficult to understand how an area so far away and so outside everyday American experience could enlist such massive American involvement. There are at least two partial reasons given, and time has shown both of them to be myths, though they seemed very real in the 1950s and 60s.

The first reason concerns the "domino theory" of international communism, as set forth in early 1954 by President Eisenhower. This theory suggested that if one anti-communist country fell to the Communists, then the countries nearby would soon follow suit. Eisenhower's Secretary of State, John Foster Dulles, saw a Communist under every national bed—as one writer put it, he "raised anti-communism from ideology to theology."

It is unimportant how correct or incorrect Eisenhower and Dulles were; their attitudes reflected those of a sufficient number of Americans, in and out of government, to stand for a majority opinion in the 1950s and most of the 1960s. Time has shown the domino theory to be false, and the growing rift between Russia and China in the 1960s revealed the united Red Menace for the myth that it was.

The second reason concerns American "commitment" to South Vietnam. The Geneva Convention of 1954 got France out of Vietnam. At this point, a largely Communist North Vietnam faced a less solidly Communist South. The "free elections" promised at Geneva and scheduled for 1956 were supposed to enable the two areas to settle their ideological differences in the political arena. But before the elections could be held, two distinct Vietnams had emerged, each depending on outside assistance. The North received help from the Chinese and the Russians; the South came to rely upon American aid. This confrontation made elections impossible, and in 1958 led to a civil war.

The reader will recall President Eisenhower's promise of aid in return for needed reforms which were never carried out. Fear of international communism elevated this vague promise into a matter of honor, which eventually found American aid translated into military support on a scale neither originally implied nor intended.

In early August, 1964, at a time when American participation in Vietnam was being soft-pedaled, North Viet-

namese gunboats shelled American destroyers in the
Tonkin Gulf, inflicting a total damage of one half-inch
bullet hole. President Lyndon Johnson, in a hot election
fight with Senator Barry Goldwater, orderd ship-and-
shore retaliation along a hundred-mile coastline—the first
American bombing of North Vietnam. This reaction was
so rapid as to raise charges that the destroyers were under
orders to attract attack—charges which have not been
proven but are not beyond the realm of possibility.

Soon—almost so soon as to raise further suspicion of
prior Presidential planning—Congress received a proposal,
drafted within the executive department, giving the President a "blank check" and authorizing him to "take all
necessary measures to repel any armed attack against the
armed forces of the United States and to prevent further
aggression." This Tonkin Gulf Resolution passed both
Houses of Congress with only two dissenting votes, and
became the legal basis of the Vietnam war.

Lyndon Johnson may or may not have engineered the
original attack on the destroyers. There is no doubt, however, of his role in escalating the war, using the powers
vested in him as Commander-in-Chief of the armed forces
and under the blanket authority of the Tonkin Gulf Resolution. There is also no doubt of Congressional involvement
in the original escalation—witness the vote on the Resolution itself. And, despite its complacency on the Tonkin
Gulf crisis, the Congress could later have slowed the war
to a standstill by refusing to appropriate funds for it, but
did not choose to do so.

A Word
in Conclusion

It's an odd thing but when you tell someone the true facts of a mythical tale they are indignant not with the teller but with you. They don't *want* to have their ideas upset. It rouses some vague uneasiness in them, I think, and they resent it. So they reject it and refuse to think about it. If they were merely indifferent it would be natural and understandable. But it is much stronger than that, much more positive. They are annoyed.

Very odd, isn't it?

—Josephine Tey,
Daughter of Time

We started out, you will remember, with a question: if the facts are known, why aren't they reported accurately in most history books? As we have seen, there are many personal, sectional, economic, and political reasons why history has been distorted. The process of historical revisionism has helped to counterbalance some of the excesses, but myths survive in spite of the truth. Many are just as popular today as they ever were.

It is easy to see how incidents would be distorted at the time, but why do people today continue to believe a myth when the truth is easily available? Is it simply stubborn patriotism, refusing to let go of a comfortable lie? Or is it something else?

FURTHER READING

The writer of a short book owes much to those who have produced longer ones in the same area. The reader who would like to know more about myths in American history will find the following books very useful:

BAILEY, THOMAS A. *Probing America's Past: A Critical Examination of Major Myths and Misconceptions.* 2 vols. Lexington, Mass.: D. C. Heath and Company, 1973.

BETTMANN, OTTO L. *The Good Old Days—They Were Terrible.* New York: Random House, 1974.

CORDS, NICHOLAS, and GERSTER, PATRICK, eds. *Myth and the American Experience.* 2 vols. New York: Glencoe Press, 1973.

INDEX